*On the Cave
of the Nymphs in
the Odyssey*

By
Porphyry
& Thomas Taylor

Copyright © 2021 Lamp of Trismegistus. All rights reserved. No part of this publication may be reproduced or transmitted in any form or by any means, electronic or mechanical, including photocopying, recording, or by any information storage and retrieval system, without permission in writing from Lamp of Trismegistus. Reviewers may quote brief passages.

ISBN: 978-1-63118-505-2

Esoteric Classics

Other Books in this Series and Related Titles

The Hymns of Hermes by G. R. S. Mead (978-1-63118-405-5)

The Devil in Love by Jacques Cazotte (978–1–63118–499–4)

Gnosis of the Mind by G. R. S. Mead (978-1-63118-408-6)

Plato and Platonism and Related Esoteric Essays by various (978-1-63118-432-1)

Clairvoyance and Psychic Abilities by A Besant &c (978-1-63118-403-1)

The Book of Wisdom of Solomon by King Solomon (978-1-63118-502-1)

A Collection of Early Writings on Astral Travel (978-1-63118-477-2)

The Smoky God or A Voyage to the Inner World by Emerson (978-1-63118-423-9)

Catholicism, Yoga and Hinduism by Hartmann &c (978-1-63118-478-9)

The Golden Verses of Pythagoras: Five Translations (978-1-63118-479-6)

Tao Te Ching & Commentary by Lao Tzu & C Johnston (978-1-63118-495-6)

The Magician's Heavenly Chaos by Thomas Vaughan (978-1-63118-500-7)

The Hymn of Jesus by G. R. S. Mead (978-1-63118-492-5)

Paracelsus, the Four Elements and Their Spirits by M P Hall (978-1-63118-400-0)

Rosicrucian Rules, Secret Signs, Codes and Symbols by various (978-1-63118-488-8)

The Sepher Yetzirah and the Qabalah by M P Hall (978-1-63118-481-9)

History and Teachings of the Rosicrucians by W W Westcott &c (978-1-63118-487-1)

The Feminine Occult by various authors (978-1-63118-711-7)

The Machinery of the Mind by Dion Fortune (978-1-63118-451-2)

Brothers & Builders by Joseph Fort Newton (978-1-63118-506-9)

The Leadbeater Reader: A Selection of Occult Essays (978-1-63118-483-3)

Audio versions are also available on Audible, Amazon and Apple

Other Books in this Series and Related Titles

Alchemy in the Nineteenth Century by Helena P. Blavatsky (978-1-63118-446-8)

Atlantis, the Gods of Antiquity and the Myth of the Dying God (978–1–63118–498–7)

The Mysteries of Freemasonry & the Druids by M P Hall &c (978-1-63118-444-4)

The Rosicrucian Chemical Marriage by Christian Rosenkreuz (978-1-63118-458-1)

Ancient Mysteries and Secret Societies by M P Hall (978-1-63118-410-9)

Masonic and Rosicrucian History by M P Hall & H Voorhis (978-1-63118-486-4)

History, Analysis and Secret Tradition of the Tarot by Hall &c (978-1-63118-445-1)

The First and Second Gospels of the Infancy of Jesus Christ by Thomas and James (978-1-63118-415-4)

The Kabbalah of Masonry & Related Writings by E Levi &c (978-1-63118-453-6)

The Poem of Hashish by A Crowley & C Baudelaire (978-1-63118-484-0)

Crystal Vision Through Crystal Gazing by Frater Achad (978-1-63118-455-0)

Fortune-Telling with Dice by Astra Cielo (978-1-63118-466-6)

The Human Aura: Astral Colors and Thought Forms (978-1-63118-419-2)

A Collection of Fiction and Essays by Occult Writers on Supernatural and Metaphysical Subjects by various (978–1–63118–510–6)

Cloud Upon the Sanctuary by Waite & K Eckartshausen (978-1-63118-438-3)

The Secrets of Enoch by Enoch (978-1-63118-449-9)

Magical Essays and Instructions by Florence Farr (978-1-63118-418-5)

The Path of Light: A Manual of Maha-Yana Buddhism (978-1-63118-471-0)

Arcane Formulas or Mental Alchemy by W W Atkinson (978-1-63118-459-8)

The Janeites, The Man Who Would Be King and Other Stories of Freemasonry by Rudyard Kipling (978–1–63118–480–2)

Audio versions are also available on Audible, Amazon and Apple

Table of Contents

Introduction…7

On the Cave of the Nymphs in the Odyssey

Part I…9
Part II…13
Part III…15
Part IV…17
Part V…19
Part VI…20
Part VII…22
Part VIII…25
Part IX…26
Part X…27
Part XI…28
Part XII…30
Part XIII…32
Part XIV…35
Part XV…36
Part XVI…38
Part XVII…39
Part XVIII…40

INTRODUCTION

The word "esoteric" can be difficult to define. Esotericism in general can be seen less as a system of beliefs and more as a category, which encompasses numerous, different systems of beliefs. It's a bit of juxtaposition, since the word "esoteric" indicates something that few people know about, while the term itself broadly covers numerous philosophies, practices, areas of study and belief systems.

In a greater sense, Esotericism acts as a storehouse for secret knowledge, which is often considered ancient (*by tradition, if not by fact*), passed down from generation to generation, in private. At various times in history, simply possessing the knowledge of some of these subjects, was considered illegal and a jailable offence, if discovered. This usually included such general topics as Alchemy, Pharmacology, Qabalah, Hermeticism, Occultism, Ceremonial Magic, Astrology, Divination, Rosicrucianism and so on. Collectively, these areas of study were often referred to as the esoteric sciences.

Sometimes, the outer garment of a subject isn't esoteric, while what is hidden beneath it, is. As an example, Freemasonry isn't necessarily esoteric by nature (at *least not anymore*), but certain signs, passwords and handshakes given to the candidate during their initiation, are in fact, esoteric, in the sense that they are hidden from the general public.

Today, in the twenty-first century, such topics are readily available at bookstores across the country, and numerous mainsteam publishers offer beginners guides and coffee-table volumes on many of these subjects, intended for mass appeal. Books like *"The Secret"* have turned previously arcane topics into household knowledge. All that being the case, however, it isn't to say that there still aren't buried secrets to uncover, ancient wisdom being ignored and forgotten mysteries to be explored. In fact, it is often that we are only able to further our own studies by standing on the shoulders of these disappearing giants.

Lamp of Trismegistus is doing its part to help preserve humanity's esoteric history by making some of these classics available to those students who are seeking to unearth the knowledge of these ancient colossi.

So, be sure to check other titles from our *Esoteric Classics* series, as well as our *Occult Fiction, Theosophical Classics, Foundations of Freemasonry Series, Supernatural Fiction, Paranormal Research Series, Studies in Buddhism* and our *Christian Apocrypha Series.* You can also download the audio versions of most of these titles from Amazon, Apple or Audible, for learning on the go.

ON THE CAVE OF THE NYMPHS IN THE ODYSSEY

By Porphyry
Translated by Thomas Taylor

Part 1

What does Homer obscurely signify by the cave in Ithaca, which he describes in the following verses ?

> High at the head a branching olive grows
> And crowns the pointed cliffs with shady boughs.
> A cavern pleasant, though involved in night,
> Beneath it lies, the Naiades delight:
> Where bowls and urns of workmanship divine
> And massy beams in native marble shine;
> On which the Nymphs amazing webs display,
> Of purple hue and exquisite array,
> The busy bees within the urns secure
> Honey delicious, and like nectar pure.
> Perpetual waters through the grotto glide,
> A lofty gate unfolds on either side;
> That to the north is pervious to mankind:
> The sacred south t'immortals is consign'd."

That the poet, indeed, does not narrate these particulars from historical information, is evident from this, that those who have given us a description of the island, have, as Cronius says, made no mention of such a cave being found in it. This likewise, says he, is manifest, that it would be absurd for Homer to expect, that in describing a cave fabricated merely by poetical license and thus artificially opening a path to Gods and men in the region of Ithaca, he should gain the belief of mankind. And it is equally absurd to suppose, that nature herself should point out, in this place, one path for the descent of all mankind, and again another path for all the Gods. For, indeed, the whole world is full of Gods and men; but it is impossible to be persuaded, that in the Ithacensian cave men descend, and Gods ascend. Cronius therefore, having premised this much, says, that it is evident, not only to the wise but also to the vulgar, that the poet, under the veil of allegory, conceals some mysterious signification; thus compelling others to explore what the gate of men is and also what is the gate of the Gods: what he means by asserting that this cave of the Nymphs has two gates; and why it is both pleasant and obscure, since darkness is by no means delightful, but is rather productive of aversion and horror. Likewise, what is the reason why it is not simply said to be the cave of the Nymphs, but it is accurately added, of the Nymphs which are called Naiades? Why also, is the cave represented as containing bowls and amphorae, when no mention is made of their receiving any liquor, but bees are said to deposit their honey in these vessels as in hives? Then, again, why are oblong beams adapted to weaving placed here for the Nymphs; and these not formed from wood, or any other pliable matter, but from stone, as well as the amphorae and bowls? Which last circumstance is, indeed, less obscure; but that, on these stony beams, the Nymphs should weave purple garments, is not only wonderful to the sight, but also to the auditory sense. For who would believe that Goddesses weave garments in a cave involved in darkness, and on stony beams; especially while he hears the poet asserting, that the purple webs of the Goddesses were visible. In addition to these things likewise, this is admirable, that the cave should have a twofold entrance; one made for the descent of men, but the other for the ascent of Gods. And again that the gate, which is pervious by men, should be said to be turned against the north wind, but the portal of the Gods to the south; and why the poet did not rather make use of the west and the east for this purpose, since nearly all temples have their statues and entrances turned towards the east; but those who enter them look towards the west, when standing with their faces turned towards the statues they honour and worship the Gods. Hence, since this narration is full of such obscurities it can neither be a fiction casually devised for the purpose of procuring delight, nor an exposition of a topical history; but something allegorical must be indicated in it by the poet who likewise mystically places an olive near the cave. All which particulars the ancients thought very laborious to investigate and unfold; and we, with their assistance, shall now endeavour to develop the secret meaning of the allegory. Those persons, therefore, appear to have written very negligently about the situation of the place, who think that the cave, and what is narrated concerning it, are nothing more than a notion of the poet. But the best and most accurate writers of geography, and among these Artemidorus the Ephesian, in the fifth book of his work, which consists of eleven books, thus writes: "The island of Ithaca, containing an extent of eighty-five stadia, is distant from Panormus, a port of Cephalenia, about twelve stadia. It has a port named Phorcys, in which there is a shore, and on that shore a cave, in which the Phaeacians are reported to have placed Ulysses." This cave, therefore, will not be entirely an Homeric fiction. But whether the poet describes it as it really is, or whether he has added something to it of his own invention, nevertheless the same inquiries remain; whether the intention of the poet is investigated, or of those who founded the cave. For, neither did the ancients establish temples without fabulous symbols, nor does Homer rashly narrate the particulars pertaining to things of this kind. But how much the more anyone endeavours to show that this description of the cave is not an Homeric fiction, but prior to Homer was consecrated to the Gods, by so much the more will this consecrated cave be found to be full of ancient wisdom. And on this account it deserves to be investigated, and it is requisite that its symbolical consecration should be amply unfolded into light.

Part 2

The ancients, indeed, very properly consecrated a cave to the world, whether assumed collectively, according to the whole of itself, or separately, according to its parts. Hence they considered earth as a symbol of that matter of which the world consists; on which account some thought that matter and earth are the same; through the cave indicating the world, which was generated from matter. For caves are, for the most part, spontaneous productions, and connascent with the earth, being comprehended by one uniform mass of stone; the interior parts of which are concave, but the exterior parts are extended over an indefinite portion of land. And the world being spontaneously produced (*i.e.,* being produced by no external, but from an internal cause), and being also self-adherent, is allied to matter; which, according to a secret signification, is denominated a stone and a rock, on account of its sluggish and repercussive nature with respect to form; the ancients, at the same time, asserting that matter is infinite through its privation of form. Since, however, it is continually flowing, and is of itself destitute of the supervening investments of form, through which it participates of *morphe*, and becomes visible, the flowing waters, darkness, or, as the poet says, obscurity of the cavern. were considered by the ancients as apt symbols of what the world contains, on account of the matter with which it is connected. Through matter, therefore, the world is obscure and dark; but through the connecting power, and orderly distribution of form, from which also it is called *world*, it is beautiful and delightful. Hence it may very properly be denominated a cave; as being lovely, indeed, to him who first enters into it, through its participation of forms, but obscure to him who surveys its foundation and examines it with an intellectual eye. So that its exterior and superficial parts, indeed, are pleasant, but its interior and profound parts are obscure (and its very bottom is darkness itself). Thus also the Persians, mystically signifying the descent of the soul into the sublunary regions, and its regression from it, initiate the mystic (or him who is admitted to the arcane sacred rites) in a place which they denominate a cavern. For, as Eubulus says, Zoroaster was the first who consecrated in the neighbouring mountains of Persia, a spontaneously produced cave, florid, and having fountains, in honour of Mithra, the maker and father of all things; a cave, according to Zoroaster, bearing a resemblance of the world, which was fabricated by Mithra. But the things contained in the cavern being arranged according to commensurate intervals, were symbols of the mundane elements and climates.

Part 3

After this Zoroaster likewise, it was usual with others to perform the rites pertaining to the mysteries in caverns and dens, whether spontaneously produced, or made by the hands. For as they established temples, groves, and altars to the celestial Gods, but to the terrestrial Gods, and to heroes, altars alone, and to the subterranean divinities pits and cells; so to the world they dedicated caves and dens; as likewise to Nymphs, on account of the water which trickles, or is diffused in caverns, over which the Naiades, as we shall shortly observe, preside. Not only, however, did the ancients make a cavern, as we have said, to be a symbol of the world, or of a generated and sensible nature: but they also assumed it as a symbol of all invisible powers; because as caverns are obscure and dark, so the essence of these powers is occult. Hence Saturn fabricated a cavern in the ocean itself and concealed in it his children. Thus, too, Ceres educated Proserpine with her Nymphs in a cave; and many other particulars of this kind may be found in the writings of theologists. But that the ancients dedicated caverns to Nymphs and especially to Naiades, who dwell, near fountains, and who are called Naiades from the streams over which they preside, is manifest from the hymn to Apollo, in which it is said: "The Nymphs residing in caves shall deduce fountains of intellectual waters to thee (according to the divine voice of the Muses), which are the progeny of a terrene spirit. Hence waters, bursting through every river, shall exhibit to mankind perpetual effusions of sweet streams." From hence, as it appears to me. the Pythagoreans. and after them Plato, showed that the world is a cavern and a den. For the powers which are the leaders of souls, thus speak in a verse of Empedocles:

"Now at this secret cavern we're arrived."

And by Plato, in the seventh book of his *Republic,* it is said, Behold men as if dwelling in a subterraneous cavern, and in a denlike habitation, whose entrance is widely expanded to the admission of the light through the whole cave. But when the other person in the dialogue says: "You adduce an unusual and wonderful similitude," he replies, "The whole of this image, friend Glauco, must be adapted to what has been before said, assimilating this receptacle, which is visible through the sight to the habitation of a prison; but the light of the fire which is in it to the power of the sun."

Part 4

That theologists therefore considered caverns as symbols of the world, and of mundane powers, is through this, manifest. And it has been already observed by us, that they also considered a cave as a symbol of the intelligible essence; being impelled to do so by different and not the same conceptions. For they were of opinion that a cave is a symbol of the sensible world because caverns are dark, stony, and humid; and they asserted that the world is a thing of this kind, through the matter of which it consists, and through its repercussive and flowing nature. But they thought it to be a symbol of the intelligible world, because that world is invisible to sensible perception, and possesses a firm and stable essence. Thus, also, partial powers are unapparent, and especially those which are inherent in matter. For they formed these symbols, from surveying the spontaneous production of caves, and their nocturnal, dark, and stony nature; and not entirely, as some suspect, from directing their attention to the figure of a cavern. For every cave is not spherical, as is evident from this Homeric cave with a twofold entrance. But since a cavern has a twofold similitude, the present cave must not be assumed as an image of the intelligible but of the sensible essence. For in consequence of containing perpetually flowing streams of water, it will not be a symbol of an intelligible hypostasis, but of a material essence. On this account also it is sacred to Nymphs, not the mountain *or rural Nymphs,* or others of the like kind, but to the Naiades, who are thus denominated from streams of water. For we peculiarly call the Naiades, and the powers that preside over waters, Nymphs; and this term also, is commonly applied to all souls descending into generation. For the ancients thought that these souls are incumbent on water which is inspired by divinity, as Numenius says, who adds, that on this account, a prophet asserts, that the Spirit of God moved on the waters. The Egyptians likewise, on this account, represent all daemons and also the sun, and, in short, all the planets, not standing on anything solid, but on a sailing vessel; for souls descending into generation fly to moisture. Hence also, Heraclitus says, that moisture appears delightful and not deadly to souls; but the lapse into generation is delightful to them. And in another place (speaking of unembodied souls), he says, "We live their death, and we die their life." Hence the poet calls those that are in generation *humid,* because they have souls which are *profoundly* steeped in moisture. On this account, such souls delight in blood and humid seed; but water is the nutriment of the souls of plants. Some likewise are of opinion, that the bodies in the air, and in the heavens, are nourished by vapours from fountains and rivers, and other exhalations. But the Stoics assert, that the sun is nourished by the exhalation from the sea; the moon from the vapours of fountains and river; and the stars from the exhalation of the earth. Hence, according to them, the sun is an intellectual composition formed from the sea; the moon from the river waters and the stars from terrene exhalations.

Part 5

It is necessary, therefore, that souls, whether they are corporeal or incorporeal, while they attract to themselves body, and especially such as are about to be bound to blood and moist bodies, should verge to humidity, and be corporalised, in consequence of being drenched in moisture. Hence the souls of the dead are evocated by the effusion of bile and blood; and souls that are lovers of body, by attracting a moist spirit, condense this humid vehicle like a cloud. For moisture condensed in the air constitutes a cloud. But the pneumatic vehicle being condensed in these souls, becomes visible through an excess of moisture. And among the number of these we must reckon those apparitions of images, which, from a spirit coloured by the influence of imagination, present themselves to mankind. But pure souls are averse from generation; so that, as Heraclitus says, "*a dry soul is the wisest.*" Hence, here also the spirit becomes moist and more aqueous through the desire of generation, the soul thus attracting a humid vapour from verging to generation. Souls, therefore, proceeding into generation are the nymphs called Naiades. Hence it is usual to call those that are married nymphs, as being conjoined to generation, and to pour water into baths from fountains, or rivers, or perpetual rills.

Part 6

This world, then, is sacred and pleasant to souls who have now proceeded into nature, and to natal daemons, though it is essentially dark and *obscure;* from which some have suspected that souls also are of an *obscure nature* and essentially consist of air. Hence a cavern, which is both pleasant and dark, will be appropriately consecrated to souls on the earth, conformably to its similitude to the world, in which, as in the greatest of all temples, souls reside. To the nymphs likewise, who preside over waters, a cavern, in which there are perpetually flowing streams, is adapted. Let, therefore, this present cavern be consecrated to souls, and among the more partial powers, to nymphs that preside over streams and fountains, and who, on this account, are called *fontal* and *naiades.* What, therefore, are the different symbols, some of which are adapted to souls, but others to the aquatic powers, in order that we may apprehend that this cavern is consecrated in common to both? Let the stony bowls, then, and the amphorae be symbols of the aquatic nymphs. For these are, indeed, the symbols of Bacchus, but their composition is fictile, *i.e.*, consists of baked earth, and these are friendly to the vine, the gift of God; since the fruit of the vine is brought to a proper maturity by the celestial fire of the sun. But the stony bowls and amphorae are in the most eminent degree adapted to the nymphs who preside over the water that flows from rocks. And to souls that descend into generation and are occupied in corporeal energies, what symbol can be more appropriate than those instruments pertaining to weaving? Hence, also, the poet ventures to say, "that on these, the nymphs weave purple webs, admirable to the view." For the formation of the flesh is on and about the bones, which in the bodies of animals resemble stones. Hence these instruments of weaving consist of stone, and not of any other matter. But the purple webs will evidently be the flesh which is woven from the blood. For purple woolen garments are tinged from blood. and wool is dyed from animal juice. The generation of flesh, also, is through and from blood. Add, too, that the body is a garment with which the soul is invested, a thing wonderful to the sight, whether this refers to the composition of the soul, or contributes to the colligation of the soul (to the whole of a visible essence). Thus, also, Proserpine, who is the inspective guardian of everything produced from seed, is represented by Orpheus as weaving a web, and the heavens are called by the ancients a veil, in consequence of being, as it were, the vestment of the celestial Gods.

Part 7

Why, therefore, are the amphorae said not to be filled with water, but with honeycombs? For in these, Homer says, the bees deposit their honey, which signifies to deposit aliment. And honey is the nutriment of bees. Theologists also have made honey subservient to many and different symbols because it consists of many powers; since it is both cathartic and preservative. Hence, through honey, bodies are preserved from putrefaction, and inveterate ulcers are purified. Farther still, it is also sweet to the taste, and is collected by bees, who are ox-begotten from flowers. When, therefore, those who are initiated in the Leontic sacred rites, pour honey instead of water on their hands; they are ordered (by the initiator) to have their hands pure from everything productive of molestation, and from everything noxious and detestable. Other initiators (into the same mysteries) employ fire, which is of a cathartic nature, as an appropriate purification. And they likewise purify the tongue from all defilement of evil with honey. But the Persians, when they offer honey to the guardian of fruits, consider it as the symbol of a preserving and defending power. Hence some persons have thought that the nectar and ambrosia, which the poet pours into the nostrils of the dead, for the purpose of preventing putrefaction, is honey; since honey is the food of the Gods. On this account also, the same poet somewhere calls nectar golden; for such is the colour of honey (viz., it is a deep yellow). But whether or not honey is to be taken for nectar, we shall elsewhere more accurately examine. In Orpheus, likewise, Saturn is ensnared by Jupiter through honey. For Saturn, being filled with honey, is intoxicated, his senses are darkened, as if from the effects of wine, and he sleeps; just as Porus, in the banquet of Plato, is filled with nectar; for wine was not (says he) yet known. The Goddess Night, too, in Orpheus, advises Jupiter to make use of honey as an artifice. For she says to him:—

"When stretch'd beneath the lofty oaks you view Saturn, with honey by the bees produc'd Sunk in ebriety, fast bind the God."

This therefore, takes place, and Saturn being bound is emasculated in the same manner as Heaven; the theologist obscurely signifying by this that divine natures become through pleasure bound, and drawn down into the realms of generation; and also that, when dissolved in pleasure they emit certain seminal powers. Hence Saturn emasculates Heaven, when descending to earth through a desire of generation. But the sweetness of honey signifies, with theologists, the same thing as the pleasure arising from generation, by which Saturn, being ensnared, was castrated. For Saturn, and his sphere, are the first of the orbs that move contrary to the course of Coelum or the heavens. Certain powers, however, descend both from Heaven (or the inerratic sphere) and the planets. But Saturn receives the powers of Heaven and Jupiter the powers of Saturn. Since, therefore, honey is assumed in purgations, and as an antidote to putrefaction, and is indicative of the pleasure which draws souls downward to generation; it is a symbol well adapted to aquatic Nymphs, on account of the unputrescent nature of the waters over which they preside, their purifying power, and their co-operation with generation. For water co-operates in the work of generation. On this account the bees are said, by the poet, to deposit their honey in bowls and amphorae; the bowls being a symbol of fountains, and therefore a bowl is placed near to Mithra, instead of a fountain; but the amphorae are symbols of the vessels with which we draw water from fountains. And fountains and streams are adapted to aquatic Nymphs, and still more so to the Nymphs that are souls, which the ancient peculiarly called bees, as the efficient causes of sweetness. Hence Sophocles does not speak unappropriately when he says of souls:—

"In swarms while wandering, from the dead, A humming sound is heard."

Part 8

The priestesses of Ceres, also, as being initiated into the mysteries of the terrene Goddess, were called by the ancients bees; and Proserpine herself was denominated by them *honied*. The moon, likewise, who presides over generation, was called by them a bee, and also a bull. And Taurus is the exaltation of the moon. But bees are ox-begotten. And this application is also given to souls proceeding into generation. The God, likewise, who is occultly connected with generation, is a stealer of oxen. To which may be added, that honey is considered as a symbol of death, and on this account it is usual to offer libations of honey to the terrestrial Gods; but gall is considered as a symbol of life; whether it is obscurely signed by this, that the life of the soul dies through pleasure, but through bitterness the soul resumes its life, whence, also, bile is sacrificed to the Gods; or whether it is, because death liberates from molestation, but the present life is laborious and bitter. All souls, however, proceeding into generation, are not simply called bees, but those who will live in it justly and who, after having performed such things as are acceptable to the Gods, will again return (to their kindred stars). For this insect loves to return to the place from whence it first came, and is eminently just and sober. Whence, also, the libations which are made with honey are called sober. Bees, likewise, do not sit on beans, which were considered by the ancients as a symbol of generation proceeding in a right line, and without flexure; because this leguminous vegetable is almost the only seed-bearing plant whose stalk is perforated throughout without any intervening knots. We must therefore admit, that honeycombs and bees are appropriate and common symbols of the aquatic nymphs, and of souls that are married (as it were) to (the humid and fluctuating nature of) generation.

Part 9

Caves, therefore, in the most remote periods of antiquity were consecrated to the Gods, before temples were erected to them. Hence, the Curetes in Crete dedicated a cavern to Jupiter; in Arcadia, a cave was sacred to the Moon, and to Lycean Pan; and in Naxus, to Bacchus. But wherever Mithra was known, they propitiated the God in a cavern. With respect, however, to the Ithacensian cave, Homer was not satisfied with saying that it had two gates, but adds that one of the gates was turned towards the north, but the other which was more divine, to the south. He also says that the northern gate was pervious to descent, but does not indicate whether this was also the case with the southern gate. For of this, he only says, "It is inaccessible to men, but it is the path of the immortals."

Part 10

It remains, therefore, to investigate what is indicated by this narration; whether the poet describes a cavern which was in reality consecrated by others, or whether it is an enigma of his own invention. Since, however, a cavern is an image and symbol of the world, as Numenius and his familiar Cronius assert, there are two extremities in the heavens, *viz.*, the winter tropic, than which nothing is more southern, and the summer tropic, than which nothing is more northern. But the summer tropic is in Cancer, and the winter tropic in Capricorn. And since Cancer is nearest to us, it is very properly attributed to the Moon, which is the nearest of all the heavenly bodies to the earth. But as the southern pole by its great distance is invisible to us, hence Capricorn is attributed to Saturn, the highest and most remote of all the planets. Again, the signs from Cancer to Capricorn are situated in the following order: and the first of these is Leo, which is the house of the Sun; afterwards Virgo, which is the house of Mercury; Libra, the house of Venus; Scorpio, of Mars; Sagittarius, of Jupiter; and Capricorn, of Saturn. But from Capricorn in an inverse order Aquarius is attributed to Saturn; Pisces to Jupiter; Aries to Mars; Taurus to Venus; Gemini to Mercury; and in the last place Cancer to the Moon.

Part 11

Theologists therefore assert, that these two gates are Cancer and Capricorn; but Plato calls them entrances. And of these, theologists say, that Cancer is the gate through which souls descend; but Capricorn that through which they ascend. Cancer is indeed northern, and adapted to descent; but Capricorn is southern, and adapted to ascent. The northern parts, likewise, pertain to souls descending into generation. And the gates of the cavern which are turned to the north are rightly said to be pervious to the descent of men; but the southern gates are not the avenues of the Gods, but of souls ascending to the Gods. On this account, the poet does not say that they are the avenues of the Gods, but of immortals; this appellation being also common to our souls, which are *per se,* or essentially, immortal. It is said that Parmenides mentions these two gates in his treatise "On the Nature of Things", as likewise that they are not unknown to the Romans and Egyptians. For the Romans celebrate their Saturnalia when the Sun is in Capricorn, and during this festivity, slaves wear the shoes of those that are free, and all things are distributed among them in common; the legislator obscurely signifying by this ceremony that through this gate of the heavens, those who are now born slaves will be liberated through the Saturnian festival, and the house attributed to Saturn, *i.e.,* Capricorn, when they live again and return to the fountain of life. Since, however, the path from Capricorn is adapted to ascent, hence the Romans denominate that month in which the Sun, turning from Capricorn to the east, directs his course to the north, Januanus, or January, from *janua,* a gate. But with the Egyptians, the beginning of the year is not Aquarius, as with the Romans, but Cancer. For the star Sothis, which the Greeks call the Dog, is near to Cancer. And the rising of Sothis is the new moon with them, this being the principle of generation to the world. On this account, the gates of the Homeric cavern are not dedicated to the east and west, nor to the equinoctial signs, Aries and Libra, but to the north and south, and to those celestial signs which towards the south are most southerly, and, towards the north are most northerly; because this cave was sacred to souis and aquatic nymphs. But these places are adapted to souls descending into generation, and afterwards separating themselves from it. Hence, a place near to the equinoctial circle was assigned to Mithra as an appropriate seat. And on this account he bears the sword of Aries, which is a martial sign. He is likewise carried in the Bull, which is the sign of Venus. For Mithra. as well as the Bull, is the Demiurgus and lord of generation. But he is placed near the equinoctial circle, having the northern parts on his right hand, and the southern on his left. They likewise arranged towards the south the southern hemisphere because it is hot; but the northern hemisphere towards the north, through the coldness of the north wind.

Part 12

The ancients, likewise, very reasonably connected winds with souls proceeding into generation, and again separating themselves from it, because, as some think, souls attract a spirit, and have a pneumatic essence. But the north wind is adapted to souls falling into generation; and, on this account, the northern blasts refresh those who are dying, and when they can scarcely draw their breath. On the contrary the southern gales dissolve life. For the north wind, indeed, from its superior coldness, congeals (as it were the animal life), and retains it in the frigidity of terrene generation. But the south wind, being hot, dissolves this life, and sends it upward to the heat of a divine nature. Since, however, our terrene habitation is more northern, it is proper that souls which are born in it should be familiar with the north wind; but those that exchange this life for a better, with the south wind. This also is the cause why the north wind is, at its commencement, great; but the south wind, at its termination. For the former is situated directly over the inhabitants of the northern part of the globe, but the latter is at a great distance from them; and the blast from places very remote, is more tardy than from such as are near. But when it is coacervated, then it blows abundantly and with vigour. Since, however, souls proceed into generation through the northern gate, hence this wind is said to be amatory. For, as the poet says,

> "Boreas, enamour'd of the sprightly train,
> Conceal'd his godhead in a flowing mane.
> With voice dissembled to his loves he neighed,
> And coursed the dappled beauties o'er the mead;
> Hence sprung twelve others of unrivalled kind,
> Swift as their mother mares, and father wind."

It is also said, that Boreas ravished Orithya, from whom he begot Zetis and Calais. But as the south is attributed to the Gods, hence, when the Sun is at its meridian, the curtains in temples are drawn before the statues of the Gods; in consequence of observing the Homeric precept: "That it is not lawful for men to enter temples when the Sun is inclined to the south, for this is the path of the immortals. Hence, when the God is at his meridian altitude, the ancients placed a symbol of midday and of the south in the gates of the temples, and on this account, in other gates also, it was not lawful to speak at all times, because gates were considered as sacred. Hence, too, the Pythagoreans, and the wise men among the Egyptians, forbade speaking while passing through doors or gates; for then they venerated in silence that God who is the principle of wholes (and, therefore, of all things).

Part 13

Homer, likewise, knew that gates are sacred, as is evident from his representing Oeneus, when supplicating, shaking the gate:

"The gates he shakes, and supplicates the son."

He also knew the gates of the heavens which are committed to the guardianship of the hours; which gates originate in cloudy places, and are opened and shut by the clouds. For he says:

"Whether dense clouds they close, or wide unfold."

And on this account these gates omit a bellowing sound, because thunders roar through the clouds:

"Heaven's gates spontaneous open to the powers;
Heaven's bellowing portals, guarded by the Hours."

He likewise elsewhere speaks of the gates of the Sun, signifying by these Cancer and Capricorn, for the Sun proceeds as far as to these signs, when he descends from the north to the south, and from thence ascends again to the northern parts. But Capricorn and Cancer are situated about the galaxy, being allotted the extremities of this circle; Cancer indeed the northern, but Capricorn the southern extremity of it. According to Pythagoras, also, *the people of dreams.* are the souls which are said to be collected in the galaxy, this circle being so called from the milk with which souls are nourished when they fall into generation. Hence, those who evocate departed souls, sacrifice to them by a libation of milk mingled with honey; because, through the allurements of sweetness they will proceed into generation: with the birth of man, milk being naturally produced.

Farther still, the southern regions produce small bodies; for it is usual with heat to attenuate them in the greatest degree. But all bodies generated in the north are large, as is evident in the Celtae, the Thracians and the Scythians; and these regions are humid, and abound with pastures. For the word Boreas is derived from Βορα, which signifies nutriment. Hence, also, the wind which blows from a land abounding in nutriment, is called Βορρας, as being of a nutritive nature. From these causes, therefore, the northern parts are adapted to the mortal tribe, and to souls that fail into the realms of generation. But the southern parts are adapted to that which is immortal, just as the eastern parts of the world are attributed to the Gods, but the western to daemons. For, in consequence of nature originating from diversity, the ancients everywhere made that which has a twofold entrance to be a symbol of the nature of things. For the progression is either through that which is intelligible or through that which is sensible. And if through that which is sensible, it is either through the sphere of the fixed stars, or through the sphere of the planets. And again, it is either through an immortal, or through a mortal progression. One centre likewise is above, but the other beneath the earth; and the one is eastern, but the other western. Thus, too, some parts of the world are situated on the left, but others on the right hand; and night is opposed to day. On this account, also, harmony consists of and *proceeds* through contraries. Plato also says that there are two openings one of which affords a passage to souls ascending to the heavens, but the other to souls descending to the earth. And according to theologians, the Sun and Moon are the gates of souls, which ascend through the Sun, and descend through the Moon. With Homer likewise, there are two tubs,

> "From which the lot of every one he fills
> Blessings to these, to those distributes ills."

But Plato in the *Gorgias* by tubs intends to signify souls, some of which are malefic, but others beneficent; and some which are rational, but others irrational. Souls, however, are (analogous to,) tubs, because they contain in themselves energies and habits, as in a vessel. In Hesiod, too, we find one tub closed, but the other opened by Pleasure, who scatters its contents everywhere, Hope alone remaining behind. For in those things in which a depraved soul, being dispersed about matter, deserts the proper order of its essence, in all these it is accustomed to feed itself with (the pleasing prospects of) auspicious hope.

Part 14

Since, therefore, every twofold entrance is a symbol of nature, this Homeric cavern has, very properly, not one portal only, but two gates, which differ from each other conformably to things themselves; of which one pertains to Gods and good (daemons), but the other to mortals and depraved natures. Hence Plato took occasion to speak of bowls, and assumes tubs instead of amphorae, and two openings, as we have already observed, instead of two gates. Pherecydes Syrus also mentions recesses and trenches, caverns, doors and gates: and through these obscurely indicates the generations of souls, and their separation from these material realms.) And thus much for an explanation of the Homeric cave, which we think we have sufficiently unfolded without adducing any further testimonies from ancient philosophers and theologists, which would give a needless extent to our discourse.

Part 15

One particular, however, remains to be explained, and that is the symbol of the olive planted at the top of the cavern, since Homer appears to indicate something very admirable by giving it such a position. For he does not merely say that an olive grows in this place, but that it flourishes on the summit of the cavern.

"High at the head a branching olive grows,
Beneath, a gloomy grotto s cool recess.."

But the growth of the olive in such a situation is not fortuitous, as some one may suspect, but contains the enigma of the cavern. For since the world was not produced rashly and casually, but is the work of divine wisdom and an intellectual nature; hence an olive, the symbol of this wisdom flourishes near the present cavern, which is an image of the world. For the olive is the plant of Minerva, and Minerva is wisdom. But this Goddess being produced from the head of Jupiter, the theologist has discovered an appropriate place for the olive by consecrating it at the summit of the port; signifying by this that the universe is not the effect of a casual event and the work of irrational fortune, but that it is the offspring of an intellectual nature and divine wisdom, which is separated indeed from it (by a difference of essence), but yet is near to it, through being established on the summit of the whole port (i.e., from the dignity and excellence of its nature governing the whole with consummate wisdom). Since, however, an olive is ever-flourishing, it possesses a certain peculiarity in the highest degree adapted to the revolutions of souls in the world, for to such souls this cave (as we have said) is sacred. For in summer the white leaves of the olive tend upwards, but in winter the whiter leaves are bent downward. On this account also in prayers and supplications, men extend the branches of an olive, ominating from this that they shall exchange the sorrowful darkness of danger for the fair light of security and peace. The olive, therefore being naturally ever-flourishing, bears fruit which is the auxiliary of labour (by being its reward , it is sacred to Minerva; supplies the victors in athletic labours with crowns and affords a friendly branch to the suppliant petitioner. Thus, too, the world is governed by an intellectual nature, and is conducted by a wisdom eternal and ever-flourishing; by which the rewards of victory are conferred on the conquerors in the athletic race of life, as the reward of severe toil and patient perseverance. And the Demiurgus who connects and contains the world (in ineffable comprehensions) invigorates miserable and suppliant souls.

Part 16

In this cave, therefore, says Homer, all external possessions must be deposited. Here, naked, and assuming a suppliant habit, afflicted in body, casting aside everything superfluous, and being averse to the energies of sense, it is requisite to sit at the foot of the olive and consult with Minerva by what means we may most effectually destroy that hostile rout of passions which insidiously lurk in the secret recesses of the soul. Indeed, as it appears to me, it was not without reason that Numenius and his followers thought the person of Ulysses in the *Odyssey* represented to us a man who passes in a regular manner over the dark and stormy sea of generation, and thus at length arrives at that region where tempests and seas are unknown, and finds a nation

"Who ne'er knew salt, or heard the billows roar."

Part 17

Again, according to Plato, the deep, the sea, and a tempest are images of a material nature. And on this account I think the poet called the port by the name of Phorcys. For he says, "It is the port of the ancient marine Phorcys." The daughter likewise of this God is mentioned in the beginning of the *Odyssey*. But from Thoosa the Cyclops was born, whom Ulysses deprived of sight. And this deed of Ulysses became the occasion of reminding him of his errors, till he was safely landed in his native country. On this account, too, a seat under the olive is proper to Ulysses, as to one who implores divinity and would appease his natal daemon with a suppliant branch. For it will not be simply, and in a concise way, possible for anyone to be liberated from this sensible life, who blinds this daemon, and renders his energies inefficacious; but he who dares to do this, will be pursued by the anger of the marine and material Gods, whom it is first requisite to appease by sacrifices, labours, and patient endurance; at one time, indeed, contending with the passions, and at another employing enchantments and deceptions, and by these, transforming himself in an all-various manner; in order that, being at length divested of the torn garments (by which his true person was concealed) he may recover the ruined empire of his soul. Nor will he even then be liberated from labours; but this will be effected when he has entirely passed over the raging sea, and, though still living, becomes so ignorant of marine and material works (through deep attention to intelligible concern) as to mistake an oar for a corn-van.

Part 18

It must not, however, be thought that interpretations of this kind are forced, and nothing more than the conjectures of ingenious men; but when we consider the great wisdom of antiquity and how much Homer excelled in intellectual prudence, and in an accurate knowledge of every virtue, it must not be denied that he has obscurely indicated the images of things of a more divine nature in the fiction of a fable. For it would not have been possible to devise the whole of this hypothesis unless the figment had been transferred (to an appropriate meaning) from certain established truths. But reserving the discussion of this for another treatise, we shall here finish our explanation of the present Cave of the Nymphs.

www.ingramcontent.com/pod-product-compliance
Lightning Source LLC
LaVergne TN
LVHW041502070426
835507LV00009B/768